The peanut cookbook

THE PEANUT COOKBOOK

BY DOROTHY C. FRANK

Clarkson N. Potter, Inc./Publisher
DISTRIBUTED BY CROWN PUBLISHERS, INC.

Library of Congress Cataloging in Publication Data

Frank, Dorothy C
  The peanut cookbook.

  Includes index.
  1. Cookery (Peanuts)   I. Title.
TX803.P35F7 1976   641.6'5'6596   76-40971
ISBN 0-517-52883-5

 *Clarkson N. Potter, Inc./Publisher*   NEW YORK

Designed by Betty Binns
First edition
PRINTED IN THE UNITED STATES OF AMERICA

With love, appreciation, and apologies to my husband, Justin, who has lived with peanut talk and taste for months and who really always wanted a novel, and to Justy, Ellen, and Micheline, with love and thanks for listening, testing, tasting, advising, and always keeping the faith

ACKNOWLEDGMENTS

Repeated thanks to my son, Justin, Jr., and Micheline Klagsbrun, a fantastic cooking team for whom no culinary extravaganza is too much and who know when to discard as well as create. And to my daughter Ellen, my infinite appreciation for her constant encouragement and creative guidance. There are also a few friends with special abilities—my secretary and girl-Friday-Saturday-and-Sunday Meryl Davis who has worked night and day and still laughs, and my constantly ready-for-consultation cooking cousin Arlene Greendale. Thanks to Donald Mishell of Tasmania Press who printed my first cookbook, La Gourmette Violette, to Gerry Rosentswieg of The Graphics Studio, to a creative public relations consultant, Jane Kolb, and to my good friend, Jacqueline Friend of New York who came up with a marvelous idea. For advice, guidance, and comfort, thanks to Jay Stein, Norman Scheinman, Nancy Sternberg, and Alvin Kabaker. Last but not least, thanks to Dr. Genevieve P. Ho, Home Adviser—Nutrition, U.S.D.A. at University of California; Patricia McCollum, head librarian of the San Vicente County Library in Los Angeles, Rita Norton, and my recipe-testers Mildred Kahn, Doris Roth, and Edna Shaw of Chattanooga, and Cle Walker. Glowing thanks to Dorothy Chu of Shanghai Restaurant of Hollywood for her creative recipes, Lorayne Stein, Edith Scheinman, and to my many other friends whose help I'll always remember.

But mainly, it's the Peanut People! . . . the farmer-growers, the Growers' Associations, which provide all kinds of research and advice on the care and handling of peanuts, and to the other peanut organizations that do laboratory research and distribute the latest recipes and scientific data. The major ones I have personally worked with are as follows:

Peanut Growers of Georgia and Alabama; North Carolina and Virginia Peanut Growers' Associations; Oklahoma Peanut Commission (William Flanagan, Executive Secretary), and

Peanut Growers of Oklahoma; Alabama Peanut Producers Association; Georgia Agricultural Commodity Commission for Peanuts; Virginia Peanut Growers Association; North Carolina Peanut Growers Association, Inc. (Joe S. Sugg, Executive Secretary); Peanut Associates, Inc., New York (with particular thanks to Morton E. Nitzberg, Vice-President, Phoebe Alvarado, and Naomi Hacker); Peanut Butter Manufacturers and Nut Salters Association (with special thanks to James E. Mack, Managing Director and General Counsel); National Peanut Council, Chicago, Ill. (Shelia Sandy and Virginia Blair); the Peanut Journal in Suffolk, Virginia (Terry Reel); Betsy Owens, Director, Growers' Peanut Food Promotions, North Carolina; and finally, the Southwestern Peanut Growers' Association.

Contents

Introduction

This is really a small working cookbook, albeit some of the recipes, like Georgia Boiled Peanuts, might require a fast trip to Georgia to get the peanuts "shortly after they've been picked."

Peanut cookery is relatively new on the American scene, except in the Southern states where peanuts are grown. As peanuts cannot be grown commercially north of Washington, D.C., the major peanut-producing states (and those most gastronomically aware of the multiple, delicious peanut possibilities in cooking) are Georgia, which is the leading producer, Texas, North Carolina, Alabama, Virginia, Oklahoma, Florida, and now New Mexico and Mississippi. While the South has a tremendous peanut industry, actually the largest acreage of peanuts is in Asia, with India and China leading and accounting for half of the world's acreage! Used extensively in Oriental cooking but known the world over, peanuts have many names. On the continent, particularly, they are called groundnuts, in Africa, goobers, and in various other spots they are known as earthnuts, ground peas, and pinders.

The peanut plant has a growing season of 140 to 175 days. Being a legume, like peas and beans, the plant looks somewhat like a pea vine, with yellow blossoms, but the peanuts mature in the ground. At harvest time the peanuts are dug from the ground in a process similar to that used for potatoes. The words "runner" and "bunch" refer to the way peanuts grow.

There are a variety of strains: "Spanish" peanuts, which are the pride of Oklahoma, are small, almost always round, and usually sold shelled, with their redskins on. They are considered to have a lower fat content than the other peanuts. The "Virginia" type, grown in Virginia and the Carolinas, is large, grows in clusters near the taproot of the plant, and is sometimes called "the cocktail nut." Georgia and Alabama growers, who produce

1

about 60% of the U.S. peanut crop, concentrate on the Florunner variety, which is the leading type used in making peanut butter and is also widely used, for candymaking and salting.

For many schoolchildren and grown-ups alike, the word peanut means George Washington Carver. Son of a black slave, and with a somewhat mysterious and romantic background, he became a giant in the field of botany and its related disciplines, and his contributions were invaluable. Late in the 1800s, when the South was in economic distress with a blight on the land, Carver taught farmers crop diversification and ways to restore the soil by planting nitrogen-producing legumes after they had taken all the nourishment out of the soil through repeated crops of cotton. Carver discovered that peanuts and sweet potatoes would yield rich crops and nourish the soil at the same time. Alabama had particular success in this. Carver is known equally for the more than three hundred uses and by-products he discovered for peanuts and peanut shells. From the latter he made dyes, soaps, insulating boards, and wood stains, and from the peanuts themselves, cheese, milk, coffee, flour, ink.

Besides having the virtue of a very high protein content with high-energy value, peanuts contain no cholesterol. Peanut oil has a special property of having a very high burning tolerance, is brilliantly clear, tasteless in terms of intruding into or absorbing flavors or tastes, and does not spoil without refrigeration. In many countries in Europe, peanut oil is considered much more desirable than olive oil for salad dressings and all manner of cooking.

The parade of peanut recipes has grown to include much more than its early homespun American provincial dishes. Highly sophisticated recipes have emerged, and we know of many international dishes starring peanuts, such as Peanut Quiche, Hearty Chinese Oxtail and Peanut Soup, Shrimp Orientale, Gado Gado Salad, and exotic Indonesian Saté. To study peanut cookery is a delicious way of "traveling" and learning about far-off places and tastes!

While it's almost impossible to imagine Americans without peanut butter, it really was not so long ago—in fact it was in 1890— that a doctor in St. Louis, Missouri, looking for high-protein food that could easily be digested by his patients, tried an experiment. He put roasted shelled peanuts and some salt through a meat grinder. Presto! Peanut butter.

The peanut's contributions are myriad. In the face of various verbal put-downs, such as "peanut-minded" and "worth only peanuts," the peanut has endured, thrived, even put in appearances recently as "Nu-Nuts," with walnut and pecan flavor but at the peanut price! The peanut has become world renowned as a protein-packed food of amazingly low cost, delicious as well as nutritious, has entered the diplomatic arena with gusto and liveliness, and has even appeared on exotic Christmas trees, painted gold and silver and hung in garlands with true aplomb!

All about peanuts

Purchasing

Peanuts are available all year, but are especially plentiful in all categories during major holiday seasons. They are seen in vending machines, nut shops, small and large grocery and chain stores, drug stores, in fact any and every place that sells food and munching foods.

They can be found to suit almost every individual and dietary need—defatted, double roasted, raw, blanched raw, unblanched, in the shells, and always salted or unsalted. They make their appearance in vacuum cans, plastic bags, in bulk form, and in tight-lidded glass jars.

Shelling raw peanuts and roasting them at home has been a Southern tradition, but now shelled raw peanuts, usually unblanched, are the darlings of the health food stores, and appear in many meat-substitute dishes as well as in salads and Oriental dishes.

Storage

Because of the high fat content and susceptibility to rancidness, shelled peanuts should be kept in tightly closed containers and refrigerated.

Peanuts in the shell and unsalted peanuts have better keeping qualities. Freezing peanuts is the safest and best method of keeping them fresh! Peanut butter should be refrigerated but taken out a little before using, so that it can soften at room temperature.

Amounts

1½ pounds Virginia-type peanuts in the shell equal 1 pound shelled.

From the point of view of practicality and economics, if the nuts are to be used in any extensive cooking operation, the shelled peanuts function better.

Preparation

To blanch shelled, raw peanuts, put them into boiling water and let them stand 3 minutes. Drain, slide skin off with your fingers, and spread on absorbent paper to dry. Roasting will also loosen the skins of peanuts, shelled or unshelled.

OVEN ROASTING

Place shelled peanuts one layer deep in shallow pan. Roast at 350° for 15 to 20 minutes until golden brown. Stir occasionally for even roasting. Garnish with butter, then salt to taste.

FRENCH FRYING

Using a good vegetable oil, preferably peanut oil, cook raw, blanched peanuts in deep oil with wire basket or shallow oil with no basket but with oil deep enough to cover peanuts. Heat oil to 300°, add peanuts, and stir occasionally to assure even cooking. When peanuts begin browning, remove from the oil as they will continue to brown while cooling. Drain off excess oil, place peanuts on brown paper for further draining, and salt immediately according to taste. For salt-free dieters, these nuts are delicious as is.

ROASTING IN THE SHELL

Place peanuts one or two layers deep in shallow pan, place in moderately hot oven, and stir occasionally. Cook 20 to 30 minutes. Shell and sample the peanuts during the last few minutes of cooking time to assure that the peanuts are roasted to your taste.

Freshening peanuts

The flavor of almost all nuts is improved by heating them for a few minutes in a moderate oven until they become crisp. For some recipes the peanuts should be left in the oven until they are delicately browned. This browning brings out the flavor and is desirable whenever it is not necessary to keep the light color. If the nuts are slightly rancid, they should be covered with boiling water, allowed to stand for about three minutes, drained, dried on a clean tea towel, and put into the oven to become crisp.

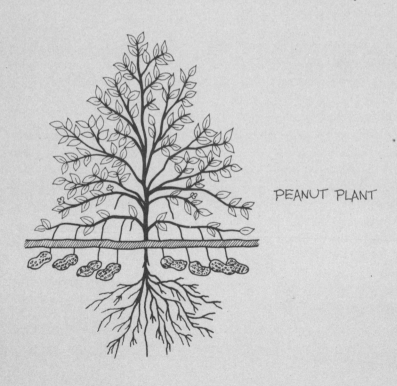

PEANUT PLANT

Nutritional information: Composition of foods, 100 grams, edible portion

100 grams equals 6½ tablespoons peanut butter or ⅔ cup shelled peanuts

	Raw, without skins	Boiled	Roasted, with skins	Roasted and salted	Peanut butter*
Food energy (calories)	568.0	376.0	582.0	585.0	589.0
Protein (grams)	26.3	15.5	26.2	26.0	25.2
Fat (grams)	48.4	31.5	48.7	49.8	50.6
Carbohydrate (grams)					
Total	17.6	14.5	20.6	18.8	18.8
Fiber	1.9	1.8	2.7	2.4	1.8
Calcium (milligrams)	59.0	43.0	72.0	74.0	59.0
Phosphorus (milligrams)	409.0	181.0	407.0	401.0	380.0
Iron (milligrams)	2.0	1.3	2.2	21.1	1.9
Sodium (milligrams)	5.0	4.0	5.0	418.0	605.0
Potassium (milligrams)	674.0	462.0	701.0	674.0	627.0

*Commercially-prepared peanut butter. Homemade or health-food peanut butter has slightly more protein, potassium, and phosphorus, and less fat and carbohydrate.

My deep appreciation to the Carter family for this recipe and, in particular, to Mrs. Lillian Carter for her gracious generosity in providing me with many delicious Plains, Georgia, recipes, including Chili Peanuts, Peanut Butter Meatloaf with Sweet Potato Frosting, Tender Peanut-Bean Casserole, and Georgia Swirl Fudge.

D.F.

Jimmy Carter's favorite peanut brittle

3 cups sugar
1½ cups water
1 cup white corn syrup
3 cups raw peanuts
2 tablespoons soda
½ stick butter
1 teaspoon vanilla

Boil sugar, water, and syrup until it spins a thread. Add peanuts and stir continuously until syrup turns golden brown. Remove from heat, and add remaining ingredients. Stir until butter melts.

Pour up on two cookie sheets with sides. As mixture begins to harden around edges, pull until thin.

Appetizers and nibbles

Georgia boiled peanuts

Wash unshelled peanuts thoroughly in cool water; then soak in clean cool water for about 30 minutes before cooking.

Put peanuts in a saucepan and cover completely with water. Add 1 tablespoon salt for each pint of peanuts.

The cooking period for boiled peanuts varies according to the maturity of the peanuts used and the variety of peanut. The cooking time for a "freshly pulled" green peanut is shorter than for a peanut that has been stored for a time. The best way to prepare them is to cook them as soon as they are picked.

There is no firm method for cooking boiled peanuts. The shells of some peanuts absorb more salt than others, so it is best to begin with 1 tablespoon of salt per pint of peanuts. Then add more salt to taste later. The texture of the peanut when fully cooked should be similar to that of a cooked dry pea or bean. Boil the peanuts for about 35 minutes, then taste. Add more salt if necessary. Taste again in 10 minutes, both for salt content and to see if the peanuts are fully cooked. If not ready, continue tasting every five minutes until they have a satisfactory texture.

Drain peanuts after cooking, or they will continue to absorb salt and become oversalted.

Pass the peanuts

Chili peanuts

2 cups peanuts
½ teaspoon chili powder
¼ teaspoon paprika

Stir peanuts over very low heat. Gradually stir in the seasonings, and keep stirring while the peanuts slowly warm and absorb the flavoring. Once they have become hot, they will remain crisp.

Garlic-onion peanuts

2 cups peanuts
¼ teaspoon garlic powder
¼ teaspoon onion powder

Stir the peanuts over very low heat in an electric frying pan if possible. Gradually stir in the seasonings, and keep stirring while the peanuts slowly warm through and absorb the flavoring.

Parmesan peanuts

2 tablespoons peanut oil
1 pound salted peanuts
2 tablespoons grated Parmesan cheese
1 teaspoon garlic salt

Heat peanut oil in flat baking pan in 350° oven for about 5 minutes. Remove pan from oven, add peanuts, and stir until coated with hot oil. Return to oven for about 5 minutes. Remove from oven, sprinkle with Parmesan cheese and garlic salt, and stir to coat with cheese. Cool and serve.

Curried peanuts

3 tablespoons peanut oil
3 tablespoons curry powder
½ cup raw peanuts
½ cup raw cashews

Heat oil in skillet. Stir in curry powder and nuts. With slotted spoon, stir until nuts are well coated and brown. Remove nuts to paper towel to drain. Serve warm.

Makes 1 cup

Peanut butter bacon canapés

6 slices bacon
¾ cup peanut butter
¾ cup pickle relish
2 (10-biscuit) packages refrigerated biscuits

Fry bacon until crisp. Drain on absorbent paper and crumble. Mix bacon, peanut butter, and pickle relish. Beat until well blended. Open biscuit packages and press biscuits into 3-inch rounds. Spoon 1 tablespoon of the peanut butter filling on each round.

Moisten edges of dough with water. Fold over to enclose filling and press edges together with the tines of a fork. Prick top. Bake in a preheated oven at 400° for 10 to 12 minutes or until lightly browned. Serve warm.

Makes 20 canapés

Piquant peanut ball

1 3-ounce package cream cheese
½ pound chunky peanut butter
½ cup Major Grey's chutney, finely cut up
½ teaspoon seasoned salt
red wine for moistening
finely chopped peanuts
chopped parsley or watercress

Mix all ingredients together, with just enough red wine to moisten
sufficiently to mold into a nice round ball. Roll in finely chopped
peanuts, or finely chopped parsley, or watercress. Serve with toast
rounds or unsalted crackers.

17

Avocado dip with raw peanuts

2 large avocados, mashed
1 chili pepper, jalapeno, or hot pepper, finely chopped
½ cup chopped onion
1 cup raw peanuts, chopped
2 tablespoons lemon juice
pinch salt
dash Worcestershire sauce
½ cup grated cheese

Mash all ingredients together and mix well. Serve with corn chips and raw vegetables like carrot sticks, celery, cauliflower, green pepper, and sliced zucchini.

Soups
and
salads

Southwestern peanut soup

¼ cup butter

¼ cup minced onion

¼ cup chopped celery

1 cup creamy peanut butter

1 tablespoon flour

4 cups beef bouillon

2 teaspoons lemon juice

½ cup Spanish peanuts, chopped

In the top part of a double boiler, melt butter. Add onion and celery; sauté until tender. Place over boiling water. Add peanut butter and flour; blend well. Stir in beef bouillon and lemon juice. Cook 20 minutes, stirring occasionally. When serving, garnish with chopped Spanish peanuts.

Serves 6

African peanut soup

6 cups chicken stock

1 cup finely ground peanuts

½ teaspoon salt

¼ teaspoon freshly grated pepper

3 tablespoons catsup

½ cup dry white wine

8 drops hot pepper sauce

Heat chicken stock; gradually stir in ground peanuts and simmer at least 15 minutes.

Add the remaining ingredients, continuing to simmer until everything is well blended. Serve hot. Add a dollop of sour cream, sprinkled with a few chopped toasted peanuts, for added glamour.

Soup with shades of India

3 teaspoons minced dry onion
1 ½ tablespoons peanut oil
2 tablespoons plus 1 teaspoon
   flour
¾ teaspoon salt
1 ½ teaspoons celery salt
3 teaspoons curry powder

¾ cup peanut butter
¾ cup milk
3 beef bouillon cubes in 1 ½
   cups boiling water
1 cup tomato juice
1 lime, sliced thin

Sauté onion in peanut oil until transparent but not browned. Stir in flour, salt, celery salt, and curry powder. Blend peanut butter into onion mixture. Add milk and bouillon gradually, stirring constantly. Cook and stir until mixture comes to a boil and is thickened. Add tomato juice and bring soup just to a boil. Place a slice of lime in bottom of each soup plate, and pour hot soup over it.

Serves 6

Sunday country chowder

2 tablespoons peanut oil
¾ cup finely chopped onion
4 cups cream-style corn (2 1-pound cans)
½ cup peanut butter (preferably
    chunky)
1½ cups half-and-half
1½ cups chicken broth
1 teaspoon salt
¼ teaspoon pepper
Optional: 3 tablespoons chopped fresh chives,
    1 cup shredded sharp Cheddar cheese

Heat oil in large kettle. Add onion and cook until transparent, about 5 minutes. Stir in corn, then blend in peanut butter. Stir in half-and-half, chicken broth, and seasonings. Heat to simmering, stirring frequently. Sprinkle chopped fresh chives on each serving, for looks as well as taste. 1 cup shredded sharp Cheddar cheese may be added 10 minutes before serving, with time enough to have cheese melt.

Serves 6

Hearty Chinese oxtail and peanut soup with French bread

2½ to 3 pounds oxtail, cut into
    pieces
1½ teaspoons peanut oil
¾ teaspoon rock salt
1 inch gingerroot
¼ cup sweet white wine

¼ cup soy sauce
1 cup raw shelled peanuts
1 cup boiling stock and 1 cup
    boiling water
1 loaf sour-dough French bread,
    split and buttered

MIXTURE FOR FRENCH BREAD
1 egg yolk
½ cup Parmesan cheese

dash of cayenne
1 tablespoon good mustard

Sauté oxtails in oil until lightly browned. Add rock salt. Mix ginger-root, white wine, and soy sauce. Add to oxtails; cover and cook 3 to 4 minutes. Add nuts and boiling liquid. Simmer, covered, 2½ to 3 hours or until oxtails are tender. Skim off fat. Serve with French bread which has been thickly covered with special mixture and then placed under broiler until hot and bubbly. If soup is too concentrated, add more water.

Serves 6

Cream of peanut soup

¼ cup butter
1 cup thinly sliced celery
1 medium onion, chopped fine
½ teaspoon salt
2 tablespoons flour
1 quart chicken broth
1 tablespoon seasoned chicken stock base
1 cup creamy peanut butter (heaping cup)
1 cup light cream

Melt butter in large saucepan over low heat and add celery, onion, and salt. Cook until tender but not browned. Add flour and stir until mixture is smooth. Gradually add hot chicken broth into which you dissolved the seasoned chicken stock base and bring to a boil. Blend in peanut butter and simmer about 15 minutes. Stir in cream just before serving. One tablespoon lemon juice and ⅓ teaspoon celery salt may be added just before serving.

Serves 6

Peas, pickle, and peanut salad

1 1-pound can (2 cups) small peas
2 small sweet pickles and liquid
⅓ cup peanuts
½ tablespoon mustard
½ tablespoon sugar
¼ cup cream or half-and-half

Drain peas and put in bowl. Put pickles and peanuts through medium grinder, or chop fine. Mix peas, pickles, and peanuts in the bowl; pour about a tablespoon of sweet-pickle liquid over it, or more to taste. Make a salad mixture of the mustard, sugar, and cream. Mix with the 3 P's.

Note: Salted peanuts can be used, but rub the salt off as much as possible.

Serves 4 to 6

Gado Gado Indonesian salad

4 to 5 carrots, peeled and cut into long strips
½ pound string beans
½ pound Chinese cabbage

½ pound bean sprouts, blanched
2 hard-cooked eggs, quartered
2 tomatoes, quartered
1 sliced cucumber

SAUCE
½ cup water
½ cup peanut butter
1 clove garlic, minced
2 tablespoons brown sugar

2 tablespoons lemon juice or vinegar
¼ to ½ teaspoon crushed red chili pepper
½ teaspoon salt

Cook carrots, string beans, and Chinese cabbage separately until barely tender; drain; refrigerate all ingredients, each in an individual dish.

Heat water, blend in peanut butter and cook over low heat only until thick and smooth. Add all the other ingredients, stirring until all is well blended. Chill.

On a flat glass dish, pyramid the chilled vegetables, using lettuce leaves as a base. Circle the cabbage, then on top, the beans; next add the carrots, and crown with sprouts. Surround with the egg and tomato quarters and the cucumber slices placed in an agreeable design. Serve with peanut sauce in separate bowl.

Peanut gondolas

peeled, ripe banana
coarsely chopped peanuts
lettuce
mayonnaise or Surprise Salad Dressing

Cut a ripe banana crosswise through the center. Split half of it down its length, slicing only partway through. Spread the slit slightly and fill with coarsely chopped peanuts. Serve on a lettuce leaf with mayonnaise or Surprise Salad Dressing.

SURPRISE SALAD DRESSING
¼ cup peanut butter
¼ cup honey
½ cup mayonnaise or salad dressing
½ cup seedless grapes, cut in half

Blend peanut butter with honey. Fold in mayonnaise or salad dressing and grapes. Delicious over fruit or as a rich surprise flavor in cole slaw with apples.

Stuffed-date salad

18 pitted dates
3 tablespoons chunky peanut
    butter
2 grapefruits, chilled and sectioned
salad greens as desired

Fill the dates with peanut butter. For each salad, arrange three stuffed dates with grapefruit sections on crisp salad greens.

Serves 6

Salad dressings

Peanut butter fruit dressing

½ cup peanut butter
½ cup orange juice
½ cup pineapple juice, or
   pineapple-grapefruit blend

¼ cup lemon juice
½ teaspoon salt
2 tablespoons honey or sugar

Blend peanut butter with part of juices until smooth. Gradually add remaining juices, salt, and honey, stirring until blended. Store in covered container in refrigerator. Excellent with fruit salad.

Makes 1½ cups dressing

Peanut butter orange dressing

½ cup peanut butter
¼ cup orange marmalade

1 cup orange juice
1 tablespoon lemon juice

Blend peanut butter with orange marmalade. Gradually stir in orange juice and lemon juice. Store in covered container in refrigerator. Serve with any fruit salad combination.

Makes 1⅔ cups

Quick peanut butter dressing

2 tablespoons mayonnaise
1 tablespoon lemon juice

1 teaspoon sugar
2 tablespoons peanut butter

Mix mayonnaise with lemon juice, sugar, and peanut butter.

Main dishes

Tuna florentine

1 10-ounce package frozen chopped spinach
1 6½- or 7-ounce can tuna, drained
½ cup chopped peanuts
1 tablespoon lemon juice
1 10½-ounce can condensed cream of mushroom soup
1 cup canned French-fried onion rings

Heat spinach in small amount of water until thawed. Drain and squeeze out excess water before putting in shallow, buttered, 1½-quart baking dish. Top with chunks of tuna and chopped peanuts. Combine lemon juice and soup. Pour over spinach, tuna, and peanuts. Bake, uncovered, in moderate oven (350°) for 20 minutes. Top with onion rings and bake 10 minutes longer.

Serves 4

Shrimp orientale

2 pounds large shrimp, peeled
    and deveined
1 cup flour
1 cup cornstarch
¼ teaspoon salt
¼ teaspoon monosodium
    glutamate (optional)

1 egg, beaten
1⅔ cups water
1½ cups dry roasted Spanish
    peanuts, very finely chopped
peanut oil for frying

Peel and devein shrimp. Slit each shrimp down the back without separating the halves; press flat, like a butterfly. Combine flour, cornstarch, salt, monosodium glutamate, egg, and water; beat well. Dip shrimp in batter, then in chopped dry roasted peanuts. Fry in deep hot (375°) peanut oil for 5-8 minutes. Drain with slotted spoon.

Serve with plain white rice. Provide mustard and catsup for dipping. Pieces of halibut or any favorite, firm fish may be used instead of shrimp.

Makes about 30 medium-size shrimp

Shrimp creole

½ cup chopped celery
½ onion, thinly sliced
½ clove garlic, minced
1 tablespoon peanut oil
1 cup cooked tomatoes
1 cup okra
½ cup green pepper, cut in strips
2 drops Tabasco sauce

¼ teaspoon pepper
1 bay leaf
1 sprig thyme (or ¼ teaspoon dried thyme)
½ teaspoon salt
chopped parsley
1 pound cooked fresh shrimp
½ cup salted peanuts

Cook celery, onion, and garlic in peanut oil. Add tomatoes, okra, green pepper, and seasonings and cook 40 minutes. Remove bay leaf. Add shrimp and peanuts and cook 10 minutes longer.

Serves 4 to 6

Kung poa shrimp with peanuts

1 cup fresh or frozen raw shrimp
2 slices fresh gingerroot
1 teaspoon dry sherry
1 teaspoon cornstarch
¼ teaspoon salt
3 tablespoons vegetable oil
1 clove garlic, split
1 cup diced canned bamboo shoots
¼ cup roasted peanuts
1 tablespoon soy sauce
1 or 2 teaspoons Chinese chili paste with garlic

Rinse and shell shrimp. Slice each shrimp diagonally in 3 or 4 equal pieces. Mix well with gingerroot, sherry, cornstarch, and salt, and let marinate for 1 hour.

In a preheated wok (an electric frying pan or your favorite skillet will do), heat 3 tablespoons oil. Swirl garlic clove over the bottom, then discard. Add the marinated shrimp, stir and cook for 1 minute. Add bamboo shoots and peanuts, with 1 tablespoon soy sauce, and chili paste. Stir and cook 3 minutes.

Then turn off flame and serve immediately.

Serves 4

Chicken with peanuts

5 pounds frying chicken,
 in pieces

1 tablespoon seasoned
 salt

1 cup peanut oil

3 chopped onions

3 tomatoes, seeds and skins
 removed

milk of 1 coconut

4 tablespoons curry

2 tablespoons powdered
 coriander

2 tablespoons powdered ginger or
 1 tablespoon fresh gingerroot, grated

2 red chili peppers, crushed

3½ ounces grated coconut

4 tablespoons peanut butter

saffron rice

4 bananas, sliced and fried

1 cucumber or tomato, cubed

1 small jar sweet pimentos

4 to 6 hard-boiled egg yolks, grated

½ cup roasted peanuts, chopped

The milk of the fresh coconut gives most flavor, but currently, health food shops carry canned or frozen coconut milk. If necessary, 1 cup canned or packaged coconut soaked in 1 cup warm milk or water and then squeezed dry will produce an adequate substitute.

Lightly sprinkle chicken pieces with seasoned salt. Sauté briefly in peanut oil in heavy pan over a moderate flame. Put chicken into a deep casserole. Sauté the onions briefly, in the original pan. When they are transparent, add the tomatoes. Cook until all the meat juices are deglazed from the pan. Pour this mixture into the casserole, add the coconut milk, curry, coriander, ginger, chili peppers, grated coconut, and peanut butter. Add boiling salted water to cover. Simmer, covered, on the lowest flame, for 3 or more hours. Serve accompanied by saffron rice, sliced fried bananas, and small cubes of cucumber or tomato (these cool off the fiery spices). Add separate bowls of the sliced sweet pimentos, the grated yolks of the hard-boiled eggs, and roasted peanuts. Serves 8

Peanutty chicken

1 8-ounce package elbow
   macaroni
⅓ cup butter
8 scallions, chopped
½ cup peanut butter
1½ cans (1 pound) stewed
   tomatoes, chopped

8 boneless and skinless
   chicken-breast halves
salt and pepper to taste
1 onion, minced
8 slices bacon, cut into halves,
   partially cooked

Cook macaroni in boiling salted water to cover until tender but still firm. Drain and set aside. Heat butter in a skillet and sauté scallions until wilted. Stir in peanut butter and stewed tomatoes. Simmer for 1 minute until peanut butter melts and blends with sauce. Stir in drained cooked macaroni.

Season chicken and cook with onion and water to cover for 20 minutes, so that it is only partially cooked. Remove from broth.

Cover bottom of 2-quart casserole with macaroni mixture; on top of this place half of the chicken and half of the bacon. Then put another layer of macaroni and top with remaining chicken and bacon. Bake in preheated 350° oven for 35 minutes, until chicken is tender and bacon crisp. If chicken looks like it is drying out, spoon a little of the broth used for cooking over it as it bakes. This dish is delicious with a tart fruit salad.

Serves 8

Chicken sauté with peanut-orange sauce

1 2½- to 3-pound broiler-fryer chicken, cut into serving pieces
1 teaspoon salt
½ teaspoon freshly ground pepper
½ teaspoon onion salt
1 teaspoon paprika
2 tablespoons peanut oil
¼ cup peanut butter
1 cup orange juice

Wash and dry chicken pieces. Mix salt, pepper, onion salt, and paprika, and rub into chicken pieces. Heat oil in a heavy skillet over medium heat. Sauté the chicken pieces until nicely browned on all sides. Cover. Reduce heat and continue cooking about 25 minutes or until chicken is tender. Remove chicken to platter. Drain excess fat from skillet; add peanut butter and cook, constantly stirring, for several minutes. Add orange juice to skillet and bring to a boil. Spoon peanut-orange sauce over chicken. Serve with plain boiled rice.

Serves 4

Chicken with peanut sauce

1 frying chicken, cut up
½ cup shortening
2 tablespoons minced onion
3 cups chicken stock or water
½ cup sherry, if desired
1 small cinnamon stick
1 teaspoon sugar
½ teaspoon salt
dash of garlic powder
½ cup peanut butter
2 tablespoons cornstarch

Dust chicken in flour seasoned with salt and pepper. Fry chicken slowly in hot shortening in a 10-inch heavy skillet 20 to 25 minutes, or until pieces are well browned. Add onion and sauté 2 to 3 minutes. Pour off all fat from the frying pan. Add chicken stock or water, sherry, cinnamon stick, sugar, salt, and garlic powder to chicken. Simmer 10 minutes, or until chicken is cooked. Remove chicken and keep hot. Add peanut butter to gravy, blending in well. Stir cornstarch to a smooth paste with 2 tablespoons water; gradually stir into gravy. Cook, stirring constantly, until gravy thickens and boils 1 minute. Serve hot over chicken with hot fluffy rice.

Serves 4

African chicken with groundnut sauce

2 plump fryers, cut in quarters
salt to taste
pepper to taste
½ cup butter
1 garlic clove, minced
1 small onion, minced
½ cup peanut butter
2 tablespoons flour
1 6-ounce can tomato paste
2 10½-ounce cans condensed chicken broth
parsley sprigs
navel orange sections
banana chunks

Wash chicken and pat dry. Sprinkle inside and out with salt and pepper. Roast on a rack in shallow roasting pan at 350° for 1 hour and 15 minutes or until leg bone is easily removed. While chicken is roasting prepare sauce to be spooned over each portion. Melt butter and sauté garlic and onion. Stir in peanut butter. When smooth, stir in flour. Combine tomato paste and chicken broth and beat until smooth. Gradually stir mixture into peanut butter. Cook over low heat, stirring constantly until sauce bubbles and thickens. Spoon over chicken. Garnish chicken with parsley sprigs, orange sections, and banana chunks.

Serves 6

Hot chicken salad in peanut butter pastry shells

PASTRY SHELLS

1 cup sifted flour

½ teaspoon salt

½ cup peanut butter

⅓ cup shortening

4 tablespoons cold water

CHICKEN SALAD

2 cups diced cooked chicken

2 cups diced celery

1 cup cooked peas

1 cup crushed potato chips

2 tablespoons chopped onion

2 tablespoons chopped pimento

2 tablespoons lemon juice

½ teaspoon salt

½ cup mayonnaise or salad
   dressing

½ cup shredded sharp cheese

¾ cup chopped roasted peanuts

Sift together flour and salt. Cut in peanut butter and shortening until mixture resembles coarse crumbs. Add water a little at a time, mixing lightly until pastry just holds together. Turn out on lightly floured board or pastry cloth. Knead gently for a few seconds. Roll out to ⅛-inch thickness. Cut into 8 circles and fit over the backs of individual tart pans. Prick well. Bake in hot oven (425°) 5 to 8 minutes or until lightly browned. Watch carefully as this has a tendency to burn. Cool while preparing salad.

Combine all ingredients for salad, except cheese and nuts. Stir until evenly mixed. Fill baked pastry shells. Sprinkle with cheese. Heat in slow oven (325°) about 15 minutes, until cheese melts and salad is hot. Serve on individual plates, and just before serving, top each with a generous sprinkling of roasted peanuts.

Serves 8

Orange peanut duckling

1 approx. 4-pound duckling, thawed if frozen
seasoned salt to taste
1 6-ounce can frozen concentrated orange juice, thawed
1 small onion, minced
¼ cup peanut butter
1 cup water
2 teaspoons grated orange rind
1 tablespoon cider vinegar
orange slices and banana chunks

Wash duckling thoroughly and dry. Rub it inside and out with seasoned salt. Prick entire skin with a fork, at a horizontal angle, to avoid piercing the meat.

Roast duck, breast side down, on a rack in a shallow pan at 325° for 1½ hours.

Brush duckling heavily with concentrated orange juice every 20 minutes, and prick skin often, too. Roast for another half hour, brushing duckling heavily with orange juice every 10 minutes, until tender. Duck takes about 2 to 3 hours roasting before it is fork tender. Remove it to platter and keep warm.

Drain fat from drippings in roasting pan. Sauté onion in 2 table-spoons of the duckling fat. Stir in peanut butter. Add water to pan drippings. Boil to loosen all particles. Stir drippings into peanut mixture. Add orange rind and cider vinegar. Cook while stirring about 5 minutes until sauce thickens slightly. Season to taste with additional salt. Garnish with slices of orange and banana chunks and serve sauce separately.

Serves 4

Peanut dressing for poultry

1 cup shelled, parched peanuts (or peanut butter)
2 cups crumbled cornbread
2 tablespoons melted butter
1 egg yolk
broth from turkey
salt and pepper to taste

Grind peanuts; add crumbs, butter, and egg yolk. Moisten with a little broth made by cooking the giblets and neck. Season with salt and pepper. Besides being wonderful with turkey, this also enhances Cornish game hens.

Spicy veal chops

6 loin veal chops, about 1 inch thick
salt
garlic powder
⅓ cup butter
1 onion, chopped
1 10½-ounce can condensed chicken broth
1 1-pound can tomatoes, chopped and undrained
½ cup chopped celery
⅓ cup peanut butter
2 tablespoons chopped parsley

Sprinkle veal on both sides with salt and garlic powder. Sauté chops in butter in a large skillet until brown on both sides. Add onion, chicken broth, tomatoes, and celery. Cover and simmer until chops are tender, about 45 minutes. Remove chops to a platter. Add peanut butter and parsley to pan drippings. Simmer until sauce is smooth and thickened. Season to taste with salt. Spoon hot sauce over veal chops. Garnish with parsley.

Serves 6

Peanut butter meat loaf with sweet potato frosting

MEAT LOAF

2 pounds lean ground round beef	⅓ cup peanut butter
1 small onion, chopped	½ cup tomato juice
2 eggs, beaten	2 teaspoons salt
1 8-ounce package stuffing mix	½ teaspoon pepper

SWEET POTATO FROSTING

4 cups thick mashed sweet potatoes or yams	¼ cup peanut butter
¼ cup butter, melted	salt

Combine all ingredients for meat loaf and mix until well blended. Shape mixture on a foil-lined shallow pan into a loaf. Bake in preheated 350° oven for 1 hour. Keep hot in oven while making the frosting. Beat potatoes, butter, and peanut butter until smooth and whipped. Season to taste with salt. Remove meat loaf from oven and spread top and sides with mashed potato mixture. Reheat in oven for 10 minutes. Serve cut into slices. These 2 dishes can also be prepared separately, the sweet potatoes served in a casserole dish.

Serves 6

Beef roll compleat

1 egg, slightly beaten
½ cup milk
½ cup bread crumbs
1½ teaspoons salt
¼ teaspoon pepper
1 teaspoon Worcestershire sauce
1½ pounds ground meat loaf mixture
2 cups mashed potatoes
¼ cup peanut butter
1 medium onion, grated

Combine egg, milk, bread crumbs, salt, pepper, and Worcestershire sauce. Soak for 10 minutes. Add meat, mix lightly. Shape meat mixture into a rectangle about ¾ inch thick.

Combine potatoes, peanut butter, and grated onion. Season to taste with salt and pepper. Spread on top of meat. Roll up in jelly roll fashion and place in buttered shallow baking pan. Bake at 375° for 1 hour.

Serves 8

Peanut butter meatballs

½ cup peanut butter
½ pound ground beef
¼ cup finely chopped onion
2 tablespoons chili sauce
1 teaspoon salt
⅛ teaspoon pepper
1 egg, beaten
2 tablespoons peanut oil
2 cups seasoned tomato sauce
cooked rice or spaghetti

Mix peanut butter lightly with beef, onion, chili sauce, salt, pepper, and egg. Form into 12 meatballs. Brown in hot peanut oil. Add tomato sauce, cover, and simmer for 30 minutes. Serve with cooked rice or spaghetti.

Serves 4

Chili with peanuts

½ cup peanut oil
2 cups finely chopped onion
2 cloves garlic, finely chopped
2½ pounds ground chuck
1 1-pound can Italian plum
  tomatoes
⅔ cup roasted Spanish peanuts,
  coarsely chopped
3 tablespoons tomato paste

2 to 3 tablespoons chili powder
1 tablespoon salt
1 tablespoon cumin seeds
¼ teaspoon hot pepper sauce
⅔ cup whole roasted Spanish
  peanuts
¼ cup chopped parsley
hot cooked rice

Measure peanut oil into a large saucepan. Add onion and garlic, and sauté until tender. Add ground chuck and brown lightly. Stir in tomatoes, chopped peanuts, tomato paste, chili powder, salt, cumin seeds, and hot pepper sauce. Simmer until sauce is thick, about 30 to 35 minutes. Stir in whole peanuts and parsley. Serve over hot rice.

Serves 8 to 10

Lamb with an Indian flavor

5 medium-sized onions

5 cloves garlic, peeled and coarsely chopped

1-inch gingerroot, peeled and chopped

peanut oil to cover bottom of 10- to 12-inch heavy deep casserole

2 pounds boned shoulder lamb, cut into 1-inch cubes (fat removed)

1 tablespoon ground coriander

2 teaspoons ground cumin

1 teaspoon ground turmeric

2 medium tomatoes, canned or fresh, peeled and chopped

¼ teaspoon mace

¼ teaspoon nutmeg

¼ teaspoon cinnamon

¼ teaspoon ground cloves

1 teaspoon salt

¼ teaspoon freshly ground black pepper

¼ teaspoon cayenne pepper

¼ to ⅓ cup peanut butter

2 tablespoons sour cream

Cut 4 of the onions into very thin rings. Chop the fifth onion finely and place with the garlic and ginger plus 4 tablespoons oil in a blender. Blend at high speed. Set aside.

Fry the onion rings in hot oil until they are brown and crisp. Remove with slotted spoon to a paper towel; add the meat to the pan and brown on all sides. Remove meat too. Turn off the heat momentarily, adding blended onion mixture.

Mix coriander, cumin, and turmeric with the tomatoes in a separate bowl. Add to the drippings and mixture in the pan and fry 8 to 10 minutes until brown. Stir in mace, nutmeg, cinnamon, cloves, salt, and black pepper. Cook slowly 5 minutes. Add ½ cup water and cayenne. Cook 30 minutes and cover. Skim off any fat. Stir in peanut butter and sour cream; cook another ½ hour covered, removing the lid for the last 5 minutes.

Serves 4 to 6

Leg of lamb with curry stuffing

5 pound boned leg of lamb

3 tablespoons lemon juice

2 tablespoons butter

1 garlic clove, minced

1 onion, chopped

3 fresh pears or 3 canned pears, drained

2-3 teaspoons curry powder

1 teaspoon salt

½ teaspoon pepper

½ cup peanuts, chopped

¼ cup olives, chopped

¼ cup shredded coconut

1 cup toasted bread crumbs

Rub lamb inside and out with lemon juice; let stand 5 minutes. In a skillet melt butter. Sauté garlic and onion in butter. Core pears and chop into coarse pieces. Add to onion mixture with rest of ingredients. Cook slowly 5 minutes. Stuff meat lightly with pear mixture; secure with skewers. Sprinkle more salt, pepper, and curry powder over meat. Bake extra stuffing in separate dish. Roast meat at 450° 15 minutes; reduce heat to 325° and continue cooking 2½ hours or until meat is tender. Baste often with pan juices.

Serves 8

Indonesian Saté

5 pounds pork or beef tenderloin

MARINADE:

1 large onion, coarsely chopped	1 teaspoon salt
2 cloves garlic	1 teaspoon ground coriander for
juice of two lemons	beef (1 teaspoon ground ginger
2 tablespoons sugar	for pork)
1 cup soy sauce	1 cup oil

36 skewers

BASTING DIP:

1 cup oil	2 tablespoons soy sauce

Cut the meat into cubes. Set aside in large bowl. To make marinade, put ingredients in electric blender and blend thoroughly. Pour over meat. Marinate only for a few hours. Place meat on skewers. To make basting dip, blend oil and soy sauce well. Pour into a large shallow dish. To keep meat from becoming dry, roll each skewer in seasoned oil before barbecuing or frying. Be sure pork is cooked until all trace of pinkness is gone. Serve with Peanut Sauce.

Peanut sauce

3 cups peanut oil	3 tablespoons soy sauce
2 large onions, thinly sliced	2 tablespoons brown sugar
1 cup water	juice of two limes
1 cup peanuts	Tabasco sauce
1 or 2 cloves garlic	1 raw onion, finely minced

52

Heat oil and fry onions until crisp. Drain the onions well on absorbent paper. Place water, peanuts, fried onions, garlic, soy sauce, brown sugar, and lime juice in container of an electric blender. Blend thoroughly. The sauce will always be slightly textured and rather thick. Pour it into a saucepan and bring to a boil over low heat.

If it seems too thick, add water, a few tablespoonfuls at a time, stirring well after each addition. Remove sauce from the fire. Add Tabasco sauce and stir. Pass with a bowl of minced onion. Indonesian cooks add trassi, a shrimp paste, to their peanut sauce. Anchovy paste may be substituted, but use no more than ¼ teaspoon.

Serves 6 to 8

Southern pork chops

4 loin pork chops
1 medium onion, cut into 4 slices
¼ cup peanut butter
¼ cup milk
½ can condensed cream of mushroom soup
1 teaspoon Worcestershire sauce
½ teaspoon salt
pepper to taste

Brown pork chops quickly on both sides in small amount of fat. Drain fat off and return pork chops to skillet. Top each pork chop with an onion slice. Mix peanut butter with remaining ingredients. Pour over pork chops. Cover and cook over very low heat for 45 minutes.

Serves 4

Wah Sam pork with peanuts

1 cup pork shredded (about ½ lb. lean pork)
1 teaspoon dry sherry
2 teaspoons cornstarch
1 tablespoon soy sauce
2 tablespoons cooking oil
1 slice ginger
1 teaspoon salt
¼ cup roasted peanuts

Mix the shredded pork with sherry, cornstarch, and soy sauce in a bowl and set aside.

Put oil in a hot deep skillet over medium heat. Add the ginger, salt, and the pork mixture. Stir constantly for 3 to 4 minutes until the pork changes color and is cooked. Add the roasted peanuts and stir for another 2 minutes. Remove from fire.

Serves 4

Ham grilled with peanut sauce

¼ cup peanut butter
¼ cup orange marmalade
2 tablespoons soy sauce
1 center-cut ham slice, 1½ pounds
black-eyed peas

Mix peanut butter, orange marmalade, and soy sauce. Spread both sides of ham slice with peanut butter mixture. Grill over charcoal about 10 minutes, turning to brown both sides. Serve with black-eyed peas.

This is a very sticky recipe to handle and can be tidied up without any loss of flavor. First, pour milk to cover over the ham slice. Cover and bake in pre-heated 350° oven for 45 minutes. Remove ham to a broiling pan and spread peanut butter mixture on top. Place under broiler until hot and bubbly.

Serves 4

Sauce for spareribs

4 tablespoons peanut oil
¼ cup chopped onion
1 garlic clove, chopped
¼ cup peanut butter (smooth or chunky)
1 8-ounce can tomato sauce
1 tablespoon sugar
1 tablespoon vinegar
1 teaspoon chili powder
1 cup water

Heat oil in pan. Add onion and garlic and cook until tender but not browned. Add remaining ingredients and stir to blend. Simmer, covered, for 5 minutes. Use as a marinade and basting sauce for spareribs.

Makes 2¼ cups

South American stew

2 pounds Italian hot sausages
½ cup chopped onion
2 tablespoons olive oil
1½ cups water
2 cans (15¼ ounce each) red
    kidney beans, not drained
¼ cup fresh lime juice
1 teaspoon coriander
¼ teaspoon ground black pepper
2 unripe bananas, cut into ¼-inch
    slices
¾ cup salted peanuts, coarsely
    chopped

Sauté sausage links and onion in olive oil until browned. Add water, bring to boil, cover, and simmer for ½ hour. Stir in kidney beans, lime juice, coriander, and pepper. Cover, simmer 20 minutes. Stir in bananas, cook 10 more minutes. Sprinkle each serving with 2 tablespoons coarsely chopped peanuts.

Serves 6

DELICIOUS MEAT SUBSTITUTES

A chef friend, endowed with humor as well as culinary skill, once said, "If you can't make both ends meat, make one end nut." And peanuts are always ready for this performance: not only do they add taste interest, highly concentrated nourishment, and enjoyable crunch, but they have special properties as meat stretchers and budget savers. Relatively low in cost, they are especially high in protein content and nutrients. Like all nuts, they have no cholesterol and have substantial quantities of polyunsaturated fats.

This group of recipes features the total substitution of peanuts, along with grains, legumes, and other vegetarian foods, for meats, providing dishes that serve as entrees as well as accompaniments and desserts. Peanuts are readily available, can always be kept on hand, and, if properly stored in refrigerator or freezer, their constant presence and availability eliminates much marketing.

More and more young persons are eschewing meat for all kinds of personal, "health," and philosophical reasons, and are turning to organic foods that will provide the necessary vitamin and mineral intake the body needs. Peanuts are a totally concentrated food. For use in cooking they have many virtues. They give "body" to dishes, and coupled with grains, other legumes, or cheese, they produce marvelous-tasting foods that provide all the food value of a "meat-and-potatoes" meal.

Creole cheese loaf

1¼ cups chunky peanut butter
1 teaspoon salt
2 tablespoons finely chopped onion
¼ teaspoon pepper
1¼ cups cooked baby lima beans
1½ cups grated American cheese
1¼ cups milk
1 tablespoon chopped parsley
3 eggs, well beaten
1¼ cups soft bread crumbs
1½ cups well-seasoned tomato sauce

Combine all ingredients except tomato sauce, mixing well. Spoon into buttered loaf pan. Bake in preheated oven at 350° for 35 to 40 minutes. Serve hot with tomato sauce.

Serves 4 to 6

Corn loaf

2 tablespoons peanut oil
1 large onion, chopped
1 cup chopped celery
1 cup peanuts, finely chopped
1 8-ounce package
    cornbread-stuffing mix
2 cups diced cooked carrots

2 cups (8 ounces) grated sharp
    Cheddar cheese
3 cups milk
⅓ cup peanut butter
4 eggs, beaten
2 teaspoons salt

In a large skillet heat oil and sauté onion and celery until soft. Stir in peanuts, stuffing mix, and carrots. Add cheese. Beat milk, peanut butter, eggs, and salt until smooth. Pour over bread mixture and let stand until liquid is absorbed. Stir well and pack into a 9 x 5 x 3-inch loaf pan that has been lined with foil and heavily buttered. Bake in preheated 350° oven for 1 hour. Unmold onto a platter and carefully strip off foil. Cut into slices and serve with any highly seasoned cream sauce.

Serves 8

Peanut quiche

2 tablespoons butter
½ cup sliced scallions
4 eggs
1 cup light cream
1 cup milk
1 tablespoon flour
½ teaspoon salt
1 cup (1¼ pound) grated sharp Cheddar cheese, lightly packed
½ cup dry roasted peanuts, finely chopped
1 9-inch unbaked pastry shell

Melt butter in a saucepan; add scallions and cook until tender. Remove from heat. With rotary beater, beat together eggs, light cream, milk, flour, and salt until well blended. Stir in cooked scallions. Sprinkle cheese and nuts over bottom of unbaked pastry shell. Pour egg mixture over cheese-and-peanut layer. Bake in preheated 375° oven for 35 to 40 minutes or until a knife inserted in center comes out clean. Cut into thin wedges and serve immediately.

Serves 10

Peanut surprise pizza

commercial pizza dough for two
  12-inch pizzas
butter
⅔ cup chopped green pepper
⅔ cup chopped onion
2 cloves garlic, crushed or minced
2 cups tomato sauce
½ teaspoon oregano leaves
½ teaspoon dried basil leaves

½ teaspoon chili powder
½ teaspoon salt
¼ teaspoon pepper
½ cup creamy peanut butter
½ cup roasted Spanish peanuts,
  chopped
1 8-ounce package sliced
  Muenster cheese, halved

Divide dough in half. On a lightly floured board, roll each half into a circle to fit a 12-inch pizza pan. Place each in a buttered pan and press around rim of pan to form a standing rim of dough. Place an inverted 9-inch pie plate on each pizza, leaving rim on outside of pie plate. Bake at 350° for 10 minutes. When cool, wrap tightly and store in refrigerator (up to 8 days). Bring to room temperature before using.

When ready to use, sauté green pepper, onion, and garlic in remaining 2 tablespoons peanut oil until tender (about 5 minutes). Stir in tomato sauce, oregano, basil, chili powder, salt, and pepper. Cover and simmer 5 minutes. Spread bottom of each crust evenly with half the creamy peanut butter and sprinkle each with half the chopped roasted Spanish peanuts. Cover with prepared tomato sauce and top with sliced cheese. Bake at 425° for 25 minutes, or until brown and bubbly.

Makes two 12-inch pizzas

Peanut-stuffed peppers

6 medium-size green peppers

10 ounces (1¼ cups) grated sharp Cheddar cheese

2 eggs, well beaten

1 teaspoon salt

4 cups cooked brown rice

½ cup finely chopped celery

¼ cup finely chopped onion

½ cup peanut butter

1 16-ounce can tomato sauce

Slice tops from peppers and remove seeds. Drop peppers into boiling salted water and simmer for 5 minutes. Drain. In a bowl, combine remaining ingredients except tomato sauce. Mix until well blended. Stuff peppers with mixture and place peppers side by side in a shallow baking pan. Pour tomato sauce over peppers. Bake in preheated 375° oven for 35 to 40 minutes or until peppers are tender.

Serves 6

Crunchy macaroni

1½ cups elbow macaroni, cooked
1 tablespoon butter
2 tablespoons flour
1 teaspoon salt
2 cups milk
½ teaspoon dry mustard
1½ cups grated sharp Cheddar cheese
3 hard-cooked eggs, quartered
½ cup Spanish peanuts

Cook macaroni in boiling salted water until tender. Drain and rinse with hot water. Pour macaroni into a buttered 1½-quart casserole. Melt butter in a saucepan. Stir in flour and salt. Gradually stir in milk and mustard. Cook over low heat, stirring constantly, until sauce bubbles and thickens slightly. Stir in cheese until melted. Fold in eggs and peanuts. Pour sauce over macaroni and stir to blend. Bake in a preheated 350° oven for 40 to 45 minutes or until top is brown.

Serves 6

Surprise burgers

1 cup peanut butter
3 cups cooked brown rice or white rice
1 cup grated sharp Cheddar cheese
1 cup roasted soybeans, chopped
1 egg
1 clove garlic, chopped
1 onion, minced
salt and pepper
dry bread crumbs
¼ cup butter

In a bowl mix peanut butter, rice, cheese, soybeans, egg, garlic, and onion. Add salt and pepper to taste. Add dry bread crumbs, if necessary, until mixture is thick enough to shape into 6 patties. Coat patties with bread crumbs. Heat butter in a skillet and brown patties on both sides. Serve on a toasted hamburger bun with catsup and onion rings, or serve plain with vegetables and salad.

Serves 6

Lentil burgers with peanut butter

2 tablespoons butter
1 onion, finely minced
3 cups cooked lentils or other beans
½ cup peanut butter
⅓ cup catsup
2 cups soft whole-wheat bread crumbs

1 teaspoon seasoned salt
½ teaspoon cumin
½ teaspoon coriander
¼ teaspoon turmeric
1 egg, well beaten
wheat germ, for coating
3 tablespoons peanut oil

Heat butter in a small skillet and sauté onion for 5 minutes. In a bowl mash lentils until pasty and stir in onions and drippings, peanut butter, catsup, crumbs, and all the seasonings. Shape mixture into 6 patties. Dip patties into egg and then into wheat germ. Heat oil in a large skillet and fry patties until brown on both sides. If this is not used as a strictly vegetarian dish, the Lentil Burgers are particularly delicious on toasted hamburger buns, topped with crisp bacon. Pickles, of course! Garlic in a small quantity is optional, but good. The cumin, coriander, and turmeric can be eliminated if a spicy flavor isn't desired.

Serves 6

Peanut-spaghetti casserole

2 cups spaghetti
salt
¼ cup butter, melted
3 tablespoons flour
1 teaspoon dry mustard
¼ teaspoon pepper
1 teaspoon salt
2 cups milk

1 tablespoon instant minced onion
3 drops hot pepper sauce
½ cup sliced black olives
1 cup grated Cheddar cheese
1 cup chopped peanuts
⅓ cup fine dry bread crumbs
1½ tablespoons melted butter

Cook spaghetti in boiling salted water until tender; drain. Blend ¼ cup butter, flour, mustard, pepper, and 1 teaspoon salt. Add next 3 ingredients and cook, stirring, until thickened. Put half the spaghetti in buttered 2-quart casserole. Add half the olives, cheese, and peanuts. Repeat layers. Pour sauce over top. Mix crumbs with 1½ tablespoons melted butter and sprinkle on top. Bake in preheated 350° oven for 25 minutes or until bubbly.

Serves 4 to 6

Vegetables

Red rice pilaf

8 tablespoons butter
3 cups dry rice
1 small onion, finely chopped
1 small tomato, finely chopped
2½ cups tomato juice
3 cups beef consommé
salt and pepper to taste
1 cup chopped peanuts

Melt butter in a heavy pan and add rice. Cook until butter sizzles; then add onion, tomato, tomato juice, consommé, and salt and pepper to taste. Stir and cover tightly. Bake in 375° oven for ½ hour. Mix lightly with a fork, sprinkle with peanuts, cover and bake 25 minutes more, or until rice is tender.

Serves 6 to 8

Easy-does-it casserole

2 cups hot mashed potatoes
1 cup bread crumbs
½ teaspoon pepper
½ teaspoon salt
4 tablespoons butter, melted
2 tablespoons onion juice
1 cup finely ground peanuts

Mix ingredients, place in buttered casserole, and bake uncovered at 350° for ½ hour.

Serves 6

Tender peanut-bean casserole

2 packages frozen French-style green beans, sliced
¼ cup butter
¼ cup finely chopped onion
1 can condensed cream of mushroom soup
¼ cup chopped pimento
½ cup salted peanuts, finely chopped
1 cup potato chips, finely crushed
½ cup grated natural Cheddar cheese
paprika
parsley sprigs

Cook and drain beans. While beans are hot, add butter and mix. Add onion, mushroom soup, pimento, and peanuts. Toss lightly. Place in buttered casserole. Combine crushed potato chips and grated cheese. Spread evenly over top. Bake at 350° for 30 minutes. Garnish with paprika and sprigs of parsley.

Serves 4 to 6

Spinach with peanuts

3 10½-ounce packages frozen leaf spinach, thawed
6 tablespoons peanut oil
2 cloves garlic, split
¾ cup fresh peanuts, chopped
¾ pound diced ham steak (preferably country ham)
salt to taste
freshly ground pepper to taste

Take a handful of the spinach at a time and squeeze out the excess water. Chop the spinach coarsely, then pull the pieces apart.

Heat the oil, add garlic cloves, and cook 2 to 3 minutes; remove garlic from pan. Add nuts and keep stirring until brown. Stir in spinach and ham and simmer 5 minutes covered. Remove lid and continue cooking for another 5 to 7 minutes. Taste for seasoning; the ham may have provided enough salt.

Serves 6 to 8

Cauliflower with peanut butter sauce

1 medium head cauliflower, broken into flowerets
¼ cup butter
½ cup peanut butter
¼ cup mayonnaise
1 tablespoon sugar
1 tablespoon lemon juice
1 teaspoon chili sauce
hot pepper sauce to taste

Parboil cauliflower 10 to 12 minutes in salted water. Drain. Melt butter in skillet. Add cauliflower and sauté until light brown. Drain.

Combine peanut butter, mayonnaise, sugar, lemon juice, chili sauce, and hot pepper sauce in bowl. Stir well, spoon on top of hot cauliflower, and serve immediately.

Serves 4

Peanut candied carrots

1 pound fresh carrots
1 tablespoon butter
¼ cup peanut brittle, coarsely chopped
1 tablespoon water

Wash and peel carrots and cut into finger-size strips. Cook in small amount of boiling salted water until tender. Meanwhile, measure butter into small saucepan, and place over low heat until melted. Add peanut brittle and water and continue heating, stirring frequently, until candy is melted. Drain carrots and pour melted candy over them, tossing to glaze. Serve at once.

Serves 4 to 6

Brussels sprouts with peanuts

1 quart fresh Brussels sprouts
½ cup chopped salted peanuts
2 tablespoons butter or margarine
½ teaspoon salt

Trim sprouts and wash thoroughly. Soak in cold, salted water 30 minutes. Drain. Put into a 1-quart heavy saucepan. Rinse and drain again. Cover and place over medium high heat. When cover is hot to touch, reduce heat and cook 10 minutes. Stir, re-cover, and cook 2 minutes longer. Meanwhile, sauté peanuts in butter. Add with salt to cooked sprouts and toss lightly.

Serves 4

Scalloped pineapple
with peanuts

6 slices day-old bread
½ cup melted butter
1 1-pound, 4-ounce can crushed pineapple
½ cup chopped salted peanuts
1 cup sugar
grated rind and juice of 1 lemon

Pull bread into tiny pieces. Mix with butter. Blend pineapple, peanuts, sugar, lemon rind, and lemon juice into bread mixture. Pour into oiled 1½-quart casserole. Bake at 350° for 1 hour. Serve warm with ham, chicken, turkey, or pork.

Serves 6 to 8

Peanut and eggplant scallop

1 small eggplant
1 tablespoon butter
1 tablespoon finely chopped onion
½ cup soft bread crumbs
½ teaspoon salt
1 egg
½ cup finely chopped salted peanuts
¾ cup condensed tomato soup, undiluted
1 teaspoon horseradish
¼ cup dry bread crumbs
1 tablespoon melted butter
¼ cup grated Parmesan cheese

Pare the eggplant and cut in cubes. Cook in boiling, salted water until tender (15 to 20 minutes). Drain.

Add all ingredients except dry bread crumbs, melted butter, and cheese and stir gently.

Pour mixture into buttered 1-quart baking dish. Sprinkle top with bread crumbs mixed with melted butter and bake in 350° oven for 25 minutes. Then sprinkle grated cheese over top and bake 5 minutes longer.

Serves 4

Breads, biscuits, and breakfast

Peanut butter

1 cup salted, roasted Spanish peanuts
½ teaspoon salt
1 tablespoon peanut oil

Place ingredients in an electric blender. Blend until mixture becomes pastelike or spreadable. It may be necessary to add more peanut oil. The ingredients must be blended for several minutes. Store in tightly covered container.

Note: Homemade peanut butter will separate on standing. Stir before using.

Peanut butter bread

1 ½ cups milk
¾ cup peanut butter
½ cup sugar
1 egg

2 cups flour, sifted
4 teaspoons baking powder
¼ teaspoon salt
¾ cup salted peanuts, chopped

Warm milk. Add it slowly to peanut butter and beat until smooth. Add sugar and egg and beat again. Add flour sifted with baking powder and salt. Add peanuts and beat thoroughly. Pour into greased loaf pan and bake at 325° 1 hour.

83

Peanut butter yeast loaf

¾ cup milk, scalded
¼ cup sugar
⅓ cup creamy peanut butter
1½ teaspoons salt
1 cake yeast
¼ cup lukewarm water
1 egg, slightly beaten
3½ cups flour, sifted
butter
1 egg white, slightly beaten
2 tablespoons salted peanut
    halves

Thoroughly blend hot milk with sugar, peanut butter, and salt; cool to lukewarm. Stir yeast into lukewarm water until dissolved; add egg; mix well. Stir into lukewarm peanut butter mixture. Add half the flour; beat well. Beat in remaining flour. Knead on lightly floured board until smooth and elastic, from 7 to 10 minutes. Place in buttered bowl, turning over once to butter dough lightly. Cover and let rise in warm place for 2 hours. Punch down, cover, and let rise until half again its original size. Punch down, mold into loaf, and place in buttered loaf pan. Cover with towel and let rise until double its original size. Bake in preheated oven at 375° for 25 to 30 minutes or until well browned. Remove from oven, brush with egg white, and scatter with peanut halves, pressing them lightly against glaze. Return to oven for 3 minutes. Cool before slicing.

African groundnut bread

2 packages yeast (dry or cake)
1 tablespoon salt
1 tablespoon melted butter
2½ cups warm water in a large, warm bowl
7 cups flour
1 cup crunchy peanut butter
½ cup butter, softened
1 egg white, beaten with 1 tablespoon water
⅔ cup roasted peanuts

Dissolve yeast, salt, and butter in warm water. Stir in the flour, mixing well. Knead 5 minutes. Butter top and all around dough ball. Cover and let rise in warm place until double.

Turn out on floured board and divide in two. Roll each piece to approximately 10″ x 15″.

Mix peanut butter and butter until thoroughly blended and spread ½ on top of ½ of dough. Roll tightly and coil in circle. Brush with melted butter and let rise in warm place until double its bulk. Brush again with warm, melted butter and slash or score the top.

Bake in preheated 450° oven for 25 minutes; remove, brush with egg white beaten with water, press in roasted peanuts, and return to oven for 5 minutes. Cool on rack. Do the same with the second half of dough.

Two muffin recipes

Peanut muffins

¾ cup cornmeal

1¼ cups flour

1 teaspoon salt

4 teaspoons baking powder

2 tablespoons sugar

1 cup peanuts, finely ground

1¼ cups milk

1 egg, well beaten

¼ cup melted butter

Mix dry ingredients, add peanuts. Mix milk and beaten egg, add to dry ingredients. Quickly fold in melted butter. Bake in buttered muffin tin at 350° for 30 to 40 minutes.

Makes 18 muffins

Peanut butter muffins

½ cup butter

½ cup dark brown sugar

½ cup peanut butter

2 eggs

1 cup flour

1 cup whole wheat flour

¼ teaspoon salt

3 teaspoons baking powder

1¼ cups milk

¼ cup melted butter

Cream butter; add sugar gradually, then add peanut butter, creaming this vigorously. Add eggs one at a time and beat until smooth. Sift the flours, salt, and baking powder together and add alternately with the milk. Quickly fold in melted butter. Bake in buttered muffin pans at 400° for 15 minutes.

Makes 18 muffins

Hot rebel biscuits

2 cups sifted flour
¾ teaspoon salt
2½ teaspoons baking powder

¼ cup chunky peanut butter
2 tablespoons shortening
¾ cup milk

Sift dry ingredients and work in blended peanut butter and shortening. Add milk slowly, stirring to a soft dough. Knead a few times on a lightly floured board; roll or pat to ½-inch thickness. Cut in rounds and bake on an ungreased baking sheet in a hot oven (450°) for 12 to 15 minutes. Split, butter, and tuck in a thin slice of ham for a wonderful combination of flavors.

Makes 24 small biscuits

Dixie French toast

½ cup peanut butter
8 slices crisp bacon, crumbled
12 slices white bread
2 bananas
2 eggs, beaten
1 cup milk

Combine peanut butter and bacon and spread each slice of bread with about 1 tablespoon of mixture. Slice bananas and place on one half of bread. Dip closed sandwiches in mixture of beaten eggs and milk and brown in a little hot butter. Serve with strawberry jam.

Makes 6 sandwiches

Peanut butter pancakes

3 tablespoons peanut butter   1 egg
1 cup pancake mix   1 cup milk

Combine all ingredients and beat until smooth. Bake on a pre-heated, lightly greased skillet or grill.

Makes 12 medium-size pancakes

Granola

1 cup dark brown sugar, firmly   1 package mixed dried fruits,
    packed   pitted and chopped
1 package pitted dates, chopped   5 cups quick-cooking oatmeal
½ cup peanut butter   ½ cup peanut oil
1½ cups peanuts   1 cup wheat germ

Combine all ingredients and mix with fingers until crumbly. Spread mixture in 10 x 15 x 2-inch baking pan. Bake in pre-heated 350° oven for 20 minutes. Cool and store in a cool dry place.

Desserts
and
candies

Peanut butter pie

2 cups milk
⅓ cup sugar
⅓ cup flour
¼ teaspoon salt
2 beaten egg yolks
½ teaspoon vanilla
½ cup peanut butter
1 8-inch pie shell, baked
1 cup heavy cream, whipped
¼ cup roasted peanuts, chopped

Scald 1½ cups milk in saucepan and add a small amount to a mixture of sugar, flour, and salt. Stir until smooth, then add to scalded milk and cook 15 minutes, stirring constantly. Mix small amount of this with egg yolks, and blend well. Stir back into milk mixture and cook until very thick. Cool and add vanilla. Blend peanut butter with remaining milk in a blender until smooth. Stir this into cooled mixture; if the filling is lumpy, put it through a strainer. Pour this into pie shell, and decorate with whipped cream, sprinkled with peanuts. Chill.

Peanut butter cream pie

¾ cup confectioners' sugar
⅓ cup peanut butter
⅔ cup sugar
3 tablespoons cornstarch
1 tablespoon flour
½ teaspoon salt
3 egg yolks
3 cups sweet milk
2 tablespoons butter
1 teaspoon vanilla flavoring
1 9-inch pie shell, baked

Cream sugar and peanut butter (it will be crumbly) and set mixture aside. In a saucepan mix the next 8 ingredients and cook over medium heat, stirring constantly, until thick. Sprinkle ⅔ of the peanut butter and confectioners' sugar mixture in bottom of baked 9-inch pie shell. Pour custard into this.

MERINGUE
3 egg whites
¼ teaspoon cream of tartar
¼ cup sugar

To make meringue, beat egg whites and cream of tartar together until stiff, adding sugar gradually, beating well after each addition. Spread over custard. Sprinkle remainder of the peanut butter-confectioners' sugar mixture over top of meringue. Bake in preheated 350° oven until golden brown.

94

Frozen peanut brittle pie

1½ cups graham crackers, finely crushed
½ cup peanut brittle, finely crushed
¼ cup sugar
⅓ cup butter, melted
1 quart vanilla ice cream
1 cup peanut brittle, coarsely chopped

Thoroughly blend graham crackers, finely crushed peanut brittle, sugar, and butter. Pour crumb mixture into 9-inch buttered pie pan and press evenly against bottom and sides. Place in freezer until firmly set. Remove from freezer and scoop ice cream into crust, sprinkling generously with coarsely crushed peanut brittle between and around ice cream. Press down lightly and sprinkle remaining peanut brittle on top. Place in freezer again, until ready to serve.

Serves 8

Nutty fruit pie

½ cup butter

1 cup sugar

½ cup flaked coconut

½ cup raisins

½ cup chopped peanuts

2 eggs, well beaten

2 teaspoons vinegar

¼ teaspoon cloves

¼ teaspoon cinnamon

1 unbaked pie crust (9-inch)

In a saucepan melt butter. Stir in remaining ingredients. Pour mixture into pie crust. Bake in preheated 350° oven 30 minutes or until puffed and brown. Serve warm or cold. May be topped with sweetened whipped cream or vanilla ice cream.

Nutty sweet potato cake

2½ cups flour
4 teaspoons baking powder
1 teaspoon baking soda
¾ teaspoon salt
1 teaspoon cinnamon
1 cup butter, softened
1 cup light brown sugar, firmly
    packed
4 egg yolks

2 teaspoons grated lemon peel
¾ cup water
2 cups shredded raw sweet
    potatoes, loosely packed
½ to ¾ cup cocktail peanuts,
    chopped
1 cup dark raisins
4 egg whites, stiffly beaten
powdered sugar

Sift together flour, baking powder, baking soda, salt, and cinnamon. Set aside. In large bowl combine butter, brown sugar, and
egg yolks. Cream until light; add lemon peel. Add water alternately with dry ingredients to creamed mixture, beginning and
ending with the dry ingredients. Stir in sweet potatoes, cocktail
peanuts, and raisins. Fold in egg whites. Pour into a buttered
10-inch Bundt pan. Bake in 350° preheated oven for 1 hour.
Cool on rack. Remove from pan. Sprinkle with powdered sugar.

Serves 8 to 10

Brittle cheesecake

1½ cups graham cracker crumbs
1 cup peanut brittle, finely crushed
⅓ cup butter, melted
3 packages cream cheese
5 eggs
1 cup sugar
grated rind of 1 orange
1 teaspoon vanilla

In a bowl, mix the graham cracker crumbs, ⅓ cup peanut brittle, and butter. Press mixture firmly into bottom of well-buttered 8-inch springform pan. In a bowl, beat cream cheese until fluffy. Beat in eggs, sugar, orange rind, and vanilla until smooth. Pour mixture into pan. Bake in preheated oven at 325° for 1 hour or until firm in center. Cool in pan. Remove sides of pan and place cake on serving platter. Just before serving, sprinkle with remaining peanut brittle.

Serves 8

Peanut butter brownies

¾ cup peanut butter
⅓ cup butter
2 cups granulated sugar
1 cup dark brown sugar, firmly
    packed
4 eggs

1½ teaspoons vanilla extract
3 cups flour, sifted
1 tablespoon baking powder
1 teaspoon salt
¼ cup chopped peanuts

TOPPING
1½ cups dark brown sugar, firmly
    packed
½ cup butter

¼ cup milk
1 tablespoon honey
1 cup chopped peanuts

Cream the peanut butter, butter, and sugars. Add the eggs and vanilla, and beat until well blended. Sift dry ingredients and add to creamed mixture with peanuts. Mix until smooth. Spread batter evenly into a buttered 9 x 13 x 2-inch pan. Bake in preheated 350° oven for 35 minutes. Combine sugar, butter, milk, and honey for topping. Bring to a boil and cook slowly for 10 minutes. Remove from heat and add peanuts. Let cool and spread on warm brownies. Cut into squares.

Makes 48 brownies

Crisscross cookies

The classic peanut butter cookies

1 cup peanut butter
½ cup butter
½ cup granulated sugar
½ cup dark brown sugar, firmly
    packed
½ teaspoon vanilla

1 egg
1½ cups flour
¾ teaspoon baking soda
½ teaspoon baking powder
¼ teaspoon salt

Cream together peanut butter and butter. Add sugars gradually, and cream together until light and fluffy. Add vanilla and egg and beat well. Stir in flour, sifted together with soda, baking powder, and salt. Mix thoroughly. Chill dough. Shape into 1-inch balls and place about 2 inches apart on ungreased cookie sheet. Flatten with a fork in crisscross pattern. Bake in preheated 375° oven for 10 to 15 minutes.

Makes 60 cookies

Toffee bars

1 cup brown sugar
1 cup smooth peanut butter
½ cup margarine
1 egg
½ teaspoon baking powder

2 cups sifted all-purpose flour
¼ teaspoon salt
1 teaspoon vanilla
3 ounces butterscotch morsels

GLAZE
1 tablespoon frozen orange juice
    concentrate
1 cup powdered sugar

½ cup roasted peanuts, finely
    chopped

Cream together sugar, peanut butter, and margarine. Add egg and beat well. Combine dry ingredients and add to creamed mixture. Stir in vanilla and butterscotch morsels. Spread batter evenly into a buttered 9-inch square pan, and bake at 375° for 15 minutes. While still hot, spread with glaze made from orange concentrate and sugar. Top with peanuts.

Makes 24 bars

Chocolate peanut fingers

⅜ cup peanut oil
½ cup sugar
1 medium egg
1¼ cups flour
¾ teaspoon baking powder
⅜ teaspoon salt

⅔ cup peanut butter
1 teaspoon baking soda
⅔ cup brown sugar
2 6-ounce packages semisweet
  chocolate bits
2 cups peanuts

Combine oil and sugar, add unbeaten egg, and mix thoroughly. Sift flour, baking powder, and salt together and add all at once to mixture in large bowl. Mix thoroughly by hand as dough will be stiff. Then stir in peanut butter. Mix baking soda with brown sugar and add to dough. Blend well. Oil palms of hands to handle dough. Roll small balls (1 rounded teaspoonful or 1 scant tablespoonful each) between palms until lengthened into cylinders. Place on ungreased cookie sheets about 1 inch apart; flatten slightly with fork lengthwise. Bake for 10 minutes in preheated 375° oven. Cool on brown paper or paper towels.

While cooling cookies, melt the chocolate bits over hot water (do not let chocolate get too hot), and chop peanuts medium fine. Dip one end of cool cookie first into melted chocolate, then into chopped peanuts. Do not coat cookies more than half their length. Harden on waxed paper.

Crunchy candies

Glazed peanuts

1 cup sugar
½ cup water

2 cups raw, natural,
redskinned peanuts

Dissolve sugar in water in a heavy frying pan over medium heat. Add peanuts and continue cooking on medium-high heat, stirring constantly. Cook until the peanuts have a shiny glazed rosy look. Spread onto aluminum foil to cool. Break apart while still warm. After cooling, store in airtight container.

Makes 2 cups

Peanut pralines

1 pound brown sugar
4 tablespoons water

1 pound chopped roasted peanuts
1 tablespoon butter

Bring sugar and water to a boil. As mixture begins to simmer, add peanuts and butter. Stir constantly. When mixture begins to bubble, remove from heat and place in a buttered dish. Allow pralines to harden.

Makes approx. 24

Peanut popcorn bars

½ cup sugar
½ cup light corn syrup
½ cup peanut butter

½ teaspoon vanilla
3 cups popped popcorn
1 cup salted Spanish peanuts

Combine sugar and corn syrup. Bring to a full boil. Remove from heat and stir in peanut butter and vanilla. Stir quickly until smooth. Pour over popcorn mixed with peanuts. Stir to coat all particles. Pat mixture firmly into a buttered 8-inch square pan. Cool, then cut into 2-inch squares.

Makes 16 bars

Chocolate-peanut raisin clusters

½ pound sweet chocolate, cut into pieces
½ cup raw Spanish peanuts
½ cup seedless raisins

Melt chocolate; cool slightly. Add peanuts and raisins and mix well. Drop mixture by spoonfuls on baking sheets covered with waxed paper. Chill until set.

Makes ¾ pound

Georgia swirl fudge

2 cups sugar
⅔ cup milk
½ 7-ounce jar marshmallow
   creme

1 cup smooth or chunky peanut
   butter
1 teaspoon vanilla
½ cup semisweet chocolate bits,
   melted

Combine sugar and milk. Bring to a boil and cook at a boil to soft-ball stage (234°). Remove from heat and stir in marshmallow creme, peanut butter, and vanilla. When smooth and blended, spread evenly into a buttered 8-inch square pan. Spoon chocolate over fudge and swirl into fudge. While still warm, cut into 1-inch squares. Cool until set.

Makes 64 pieces

Peanut butter fudge sauce

½ pound semisweet chocolate
4 ounces or squares bitter
   chocolate
½ cup water

½ cup sugar
½ cup light cream
¾ cup smooth peanut butter

Combine chocolate, water, sugar, and cream. Stir over low heat until chocolate is melted. Stir in peanut butter and stir until sauce is smooth. Serve hot or cold spooned over scoops of favorite ice cream.

Makes about 2½ cups

105

Instant ice cream

Peanut butter ice cream

1 pint vanilla ice cream, very soft
¾ cup chunky peanut butter

Mix ingredients together so that they are well blended. Put in covered container in freezer.

Each recipe actually makes more than a pint of ice cream.

Peanut brittle ice cream

1 pint vanilla ice cream, very soft
1 cup peanut brittle, coarsely chopped

Mix ingredients together so that they are well blended. Put in covered container in freezer.

Peanut brittle swirl popsicles

1 pint peanut brittle ice cream (see recipe above)
paper cups
candy sticks

Spoon into paper cups. Put a candy stick into center of ice cream. Freeze. When ready to serve remove paper cups.

Makes 6 to 8 popsicles

Peanut butter ice cream

2 egg yolks
1 14½-ounce can evaporated
   milk

½ cup peanut butter
⅔ cup sugar
dash of salt

Beat egg yolks well. Blend in remaining ingredients thoroughly. Turn into freezer tray. Freeze until frozen 1 inch in from edges of tray; turn into chilled bowl. Beat with electric mixer or egg beater until smooth. Quickly return ice cream to tray. Freeze until just firm.

Serves 4 to 6

Peanut crunch topping

¼ cup peanut butter
¼ cup butter or margarine
1 cup light brown sugar, firmly
   packed

2 cups cornflakes, coarsely
   crushed
1 cup salted peanuts

Combine peanut butter, butter, and sugar in a saucepan. Stir over low heat until mixture bubbles, then cook 2 to 3 minutes. Remove from heat and stir in cornflakes and peanuts, mixing well. Spread on flat pan and allow to cool. To keep, break into pieces and store in airtight containers.

. . . and a Christmas present for the birds

1 cup instant grits in 4 cups boiling water
¾ cup peanut butter
1 cup bird seed

Cook the grits in 4 cups boiling water. Add the peanut butter and bird seed. Tie a string to a long leaf pine cone and dunk cone into mixture, coating it all over. Hang in a tree near a window and watch the birds enjoy their gift.

Index

lamb dishes, 50—52; leg of lamb with curry stuffing, 51; with an Indian flavor, 50
lentil burgers with peanut butter, 66

macaroni, crunchy, 64
meat substitutes, 58—67
muffins: peanut, 86; peanut butter, 86

onion-garlic peanuts, 14
orange-peanut duckling, 43; sauces, 39, 55
oxtail and peanut hearty Chinese soup, 24

pancakes, peanut butter, 89
Parmesan peanuts, 15
pastry shells, peanut butter, 42
peanut brittle: cheesecake, 98; homemade, 9; ice cream, 106; pie, frozen, 95; swirl popsicles, 106
peanut butter, 2; cookies, 98; homemade, 83
peas, pickle, and peanut salad, 26
peppers, peanut-stuffed, 63
pies, 93—96
pilaf, red rice, 71
pineapple, scalloped, with peanuts, 78
piquant peanut ball, 17
pizza, peanut surprise, 62
popcorn peanut bars, 104
popsicles, peanut brittle swirl, 106
pork chops, Southern, 53; Wah Sam pork, 54
potato: and peanut casserole, 72; see also sweet potato

poultry dishes, 37—43; dressing, 44
pralines, peanut, 103

quiche, peanut, 61

raisin chocolate peanut clusters, 104
rice pilaf, red, 71
roasting, oven, 5

salads, 26—29, 42; dressings, 30
sauces, 27, 39—41, 52, 55, 75; dessert, 105; for spareribs, 56
seafood dishes, 33—36
shrimp: creole, 35; orientale, 34; with peanut kung poa, 36
soups, 21—25
South American stew, 57
Southern pork chops, 53
Southwestern peanut soup, 21
spaghetti-peanut casserole, 67
spareribs, sauce for, 56
spinach with peanuts, 74
stew, South American, 57
storage, 4
sweet potato: frosting, 46; nutty cake, 97

toffee bars, 101
topping, peanut crunch, 107
tuna florentine, 33

veal chops, spicy, 45
vegetable dishes, 60, 63, 74—77, 79

yeast loaf, peanut butter, 84

110

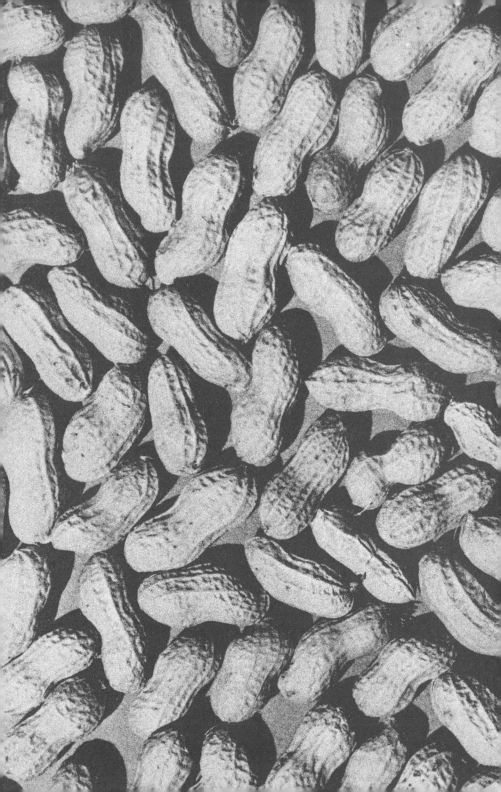